AN ALL-STAR SPORTS BOOK

SOCCER

by George Kirby with George Sullivan

FOLLETT PUBLISHING COMPANY • CHICAGO

The authors are grateful to the United States Soccer Football Association; Steve Davis, Davis and Morgan, Inc.; Jim Bukata, New York Generals; Bill Brendle, CBS-TV; and Jacques Burlot, Wagner International Photos, Inc., for their cooperation in providing source material and photographs for this book. Special thanks are due Richard Hogan, Lauro Cairo, and Salvatore Lauro who served as photographic models.

The photographs on the indicated pages appear through the courtesy of the following:
CBS-TV, pages 8, 43, 46, 60, 71, and 105
North American Soccer League, Clive Toye, front cover
Michael Quirk, St. Willibrord Soccer Club, pages 2-3
Soccer Sports Supply Company, New York, page 16
Voit Rubber Company, page 15
Wagner International Photos, Inc., pages 17, 18, 21, 23, 26, 27, 29, 30, 31, 33, 34, 35, 38, 39, 40, 41, 44, 48, 49, 51, 64, 66, 67, 68, 69, 77, 107, 108, 110, 112, and 126, and back cover.

Straightedge Art Studios, Inc., New York City, supplied the line drawings on pages 54, 75, 88, 89, 91, 92, 93, 94, 95, 96, 97, 98, 99, and 100.

ISBN 0-695-40147-5 Titan binding
ISBN 0-695-80147-3 Trade binding

Library of Congress Catalog Card Number: 71-118966

Second Printing

CONTENTS

SOCCER

CHAPTER ONE

THE GAME OF SOCCER

The goalkeeper crouches, bending forward slightly, his eyes intent upon the ball and the play that is forming in front of him. To his left, he catches a glimpse of the winger charging in, a blur of color to the man in the net. Suddenly his attacker has the ball. He fires; the shot comes hard and high. The goalie leaps, his arms outstretched. His timing is perfect, and with the tips of his fingers he deftly deflects the ball over the cage. The crowd gasps in relief. This is soccer—speed, drama, and spine-tingling thrills. Millions of people believe it to be the world's greatest game.

Soccer is the most popular game in the world. The Fédération Internationale de Football Association, the governing body of soccer, boasts that it has more member-countries than the United Nations. One authority claims that soccer is the number one sport in no less than 128 countries and that the game has 185 million registered players. (Everywhere but

North America the word *football* signifies soccer.)

People on every level enjoy the game—school-boys, college students, factory workers, professional men. It is a sport of kings, presidents, and dictators. Prince Charles, the future King of England, was the captain of his school team. The Shah of Iran is proud of his skill in dribbling the ball. And former Russian premier Nikita Krushchev sang the praises of his country's team.

Professional soccer stars are international heroes, and the salaries they command are the envy of American sports stars. There have been trades among foreign teams that carry true million-dollar price tags. The fans are impassioned and partisan, and violence at games is not uncommon. Brazil's Pelé (Edson Arantes do Nasciemento) is considered by many to be the greatest player in the game today—if not the greatest of all time. He is called, simply, "The King." His feet seem to be almost magical in controlling the ball, and he dazzles defenders with his incredible feints.

Professional soccer in the United States has experienced serious growing pains. In 1967, the year professional soccer made its official debut in the United States, not just one league but two of them operated, and this was one too many. The resulting "war" hurt the sport. The North American Soccer League operated by itself in 1968, but failed to win widespread fan support. In subsequent years, the league operated with fewer teams and less-

Pelé, "The King"

ambitious goals. The problems that professional soccer faces in the United States will be solved eventually, I feel certain. As one observer put it, "You've got to build the pyramid from the bottom up. You can't start with pro soccer and wind up with eight-year-olds playing soccer in grade school. You have to start with the eight-year-olds and end with the pro teams." In other words, Americans have to learn the value of playing soccer before they can enjoy watching it.

There are definite signs that this is already happening. An ever-increasing number of schools and colleges in both the United States and Canada are adopting soccer for interscholastic and intramural competition. Today, there are tens of thousands of active players in prep schools, high schools, and colleges; and the number is swelling dramatically year by year.

Aside from the excitement of the sport, there are several other reasons that help to explain soccer's popularity. It can be played by persons of almost any age and by both sexes. It doesn't require the height or girth of some other sports. The necessary equipment is easy to obtain and inexpensive; all you really need are a ball and a flat, open field. It's as safe as any sport you can name.

Its simplicity is another attribute. It's a game played by two teams of eleven men each. The object is to drive the ball into the opposing team's goal. Players are allowed to use any part of the body except the hands and arms in propelling the ball. (The goalkeeper, however, is allowed to use his hands and arms.)

At what age should a youngster begin to learn the fundamentals of soccer? The younger the better. My own son began at the age of five. I bought him a leather kickball, about the size of a large grapefruit, and taught him how to kick it. I also gave him a small rubber ball, no bigger than a tennis ball, to kick. He learned how to run and stop, to twist and turn, always controlling the little ball with his feet. It was better than learning with a regulation-size ball because the little ball required a delicate touch to control. As a result, he developed marvelous "feel" with his feet.

Soccer has a glowing future in the United States, I believe. Of course, no one predicts that the game is going to shoulder aside football, baseball, or basketball. But one day in the not-too-distant future soccer is very likely to equal these longtime favorites in popularity and esteem.

CHAPTER TWO

YOUR EQUIPMENT

Surely one reason for soccer's spiraling popularity is that it requires so little in the way of specialized equipment. To play the game, all you need are a ball and a pair of cleated shoes (or boots, as they're often called)—and not much else. Compared to the equipment you need for football, skiing, or golf, soccer is downright austere.

Besides shoes, a player also wears a jersey or shirt, shorts, and wool socks or stockings. But for a practice session or a pickup game among friends, conventional gym clothes will do. Just be sure the shirt and shorts you wear do not restrict your freedom of movement.

The rules of soccer state that the ball must have a circumference of not less than 27 inches, nor more than 28 inches. And the ball's weight cannot be less than 14 ounces, nor more than 16 ounces. The outside casing, the rules state, "shall be of leather or other approved materials." Manufacturers have no problem meeting these specifications; almost any soccer ball you buy will be of an "official" nature. Just be sure it's stamped so.

The best soccer balls have an outside covering that is composed of as many as eighteen leather panels, which are joined either by lockstitching or pressure molding. Some balls are waterproof; others are merely water-repellent. You can purchase a soccer ball for less than $10, but if you're buying a ball to use in competition, you should pay $20 to $25 for it.

A ball will last for many seasons if given the proper care. Keep it properly inflated. This not only adds to the life of the ball but also helps to assure that it will handle properly. If the ball gets wet, dry it at room temperature, then rub the surface with an oil-base leather dressing. When storing a ball for a long period, first reduce the normal air pressure by one half. Store the ball in a cool, dry place.

Be sure the soccer ball you buy is of official size and weight.

Soccer shoes are oxfords; they're low-cut and lace over the instep.

American soccer shoes are oxfords—low cut, with lacing over the instep. When you purchase shoes, look for support bands on the vamp, the part that covers the instep. Be sure the tongue is padded so that the laces won't cut. Remember, you'll be wearing wool socks, so you may want your soccer shoes to be half a size larger than your street shoes. Quality soccer shoes cost between $10 and $15.

The rules of soccer specify that the studs on the bottom of the shoes can be "of leather, rubber, aluminum, plastic or similar material." They must be at least one-half inch in diameter; they cannot project more than three-quarters of an inch from the sole. Instead of studs, the shoe may be fitted with leather or rubber bars across the sole. These are perfectly

16

legal, but they must be at least one-half inch in width. Some shoes are fitted with bars on the sole and studs on the heel. All American manufacturers build their soccer shoes to official specifications.

Always clean your shoes after wearing them. Wax or oil them occasionally.

If you play competitive soccer, your coach may

(left) Knee-length stockings are worn in competitive play; kneepads help to prevent injury. (right) Ankle wraps can help ward off a sprain.

17

advise you to wear ankle wraps to help prevent a painful sprain. Some coaches require their players to wear shin pads. Thick elastic bands hold them securely in place. A pair of pads costs about $4.

Goalies often wear gloves for cold-weather play.

CHAPTER THREE

THE FUNDAMENTALS

If I were asked to make a list of soccer's most necessary skills, I'd put ball control at the very top. The
ability to move the ball at will at any speed and in
any direction is basic to the sport. Top-class players
develop this skill to such a high degree that they can
move at speed with the ball, yet look around to determine how their teammates and the opposition players
are positioned. They have "feel" in their feet.

Second in importance is the ability to kick the
ball and kick it accurately over both long and short
distances. Third, I'd list trapping—the ability to use
various parts of the body to stop and control the ball
when it comes to the player at different heights and
speeds. Heading and tackling are the other essential
skills.

BALL CONTROL   Ball control is essential to dribbling, the art of advancing the ball in front of you by
giving it a series of short kicks.

You can dribble the ball with either the inside

or the outside of the foot. The inside-of-the-foot meth-od gives you greater control over the ball and is used more often.

Practice walking with the ball first, using the inside of the foot from arch to toes, and then build gradually to a brisk, loose-hipped run. Keep your eyes on the ball and your body crouched over it. Use your feet alternately in a left-push, right-push pattern. Merely tap the ball; don't kick it.

Use the outside-of-the-foot method for speed. Turn the foot in, making contact with the outside near the small toe. The ball is tapped forward with one foot only.

No matter what method you are using, keep the ball in control. This means the ball should always be within playing distance of your kicking foot. How-ever, when the field is clear of opponents and you're on the move, you can be more daring, allowing the ball to advance ahead by as much as three or four feet. But when a defensive player closes in, you'll want to literally "keep the ball on the toe."

Practice changing speed, turning, and reversing. Then practice dribbling with a partner. While one of you dribbles, the other should attempt to tackle, that is, to gain control of the ball (page 47). Then reverse roles.

To outsmart a prospective tackler, you, as a dribbler, must develop a repertoire of feints, and learn how to change pace and direction in the blink of an eye. Feints—with the head, legs, hips, or shoulders—

20

Use your feet alternately when you dribble. Keep the ball in control, that is, close to your kicking foot.

are meant to get the tackler to commit himself, to lean the wrong way. Then you flash past him in the other direction. Of course, don't seek to become accomplished in feinting until you've mastered ball control.

One standard method of deceiving tacklers as you dribble is to offer the ball and then quickly take it away. To do this, place the sole of your right shoe atop the ball, pulling the ball back abruptly. Then pivot, resume dribbling, and skim past the tackler in the opposite direction.

21

Screening the ball is another basic maneuver that dribblers use. When screening, use the outside of your foot to control the ball. This strategy enables you to keep the entire width of your body between the ball and the defender.

Changing pace is easy. First slow down, then suddenly shift into high gear.

Even if you learn to dribble as well as a seasoned professional, never forget that soccer is a team sport and the dribble should never be considered superior to the pass as a piece of offensive strategy. One of the most dazzling dribblers of all time was England's Stanley Matthews. After years of determined practice, he mastered a unique body swerve which invariably threw defenders off-balance, allowing Matthews to sprint away with the ball. Often he completely bewildered and frustrated men assigned to him. "He could destroy an opponent," was the way one observer put it. Yet despite his prowess, Matthews rarely dribbled if he had the opportunity to pass.

Indeed, knowing when to dribble, and when not to, is every bit as important as knowing how. Once in a while it may be necessary for you to try to dribble past one man, but don't ever attempt to dribble past two or three of them, not even if you feel you're another Stanley Matthews. You're inviting trouble when you do. And you should never, under any circumstances, dribble merely to display your skill. The longer you keep the ball, the more time the opponents have to plan interference.

22

Screen the ball with your body to protect yourself from attack.

Forwards must be absolute masters of the dribble. They use it to move the ball and in getting set for short passes and shots at the goal. Halfbacks do not rely on it quite so much. A halfback should always pass the ball instead of dribbling it, unless there's an opportunity to dribble in for a shot. Fullbacks rarely dribble.

23

KICKING   There are many different types of kicks, but certain guidelines apply to all of them. The principal one is accuracy. In baseball, when batting, your aim may be to merely rifle the ball above the reach of the infielders, and in football, when punting, your only intent may be to kick the ball as far as you can. But soccer is different. You must always be concerned with precisely where the ball is going to go.

Your coach will undoubtedly instruct you that every kick—except a shot at the goal—is meant to be a pass and thus must be sent on a course that is true and exact. Even a goalkeeper, when booming the ball far up the field to clear it, attempts to get it to one of his forwards or halfbacks.

Make up your mind to be accurate right from the start. Never kick a ball aimlessly, not even in the most casual of practice sessions. Always have an intended direction in mind, and a specific target you plan to hit.

The majority of people are right-footed, and kicking with this foot is simple and natural for them. But to succeed in soccer, you must be two-footed— equally skilled with both the right and left. Using your left foot may feel awkward at first, but with practice you will perform with ease.

When I was a youngster learning the game, I took a small rubber ball, about the size of a tennis ball, and attached it to a four-foot length of string. I'd grasp the string in my left hand and suspend the ball in front of my left foot, and, as I walked along the street, I'd practice kicking the ball with the instep of my left foot. In time, I became very skilled at it. Of course, once I had learned how to kick the small rubber ball left-footed, I found that kicking a soccer ball was a cinch.

If you're at all familiar with the game of golf, you know that one of the basic rules is to keep your eyes on the ball as you swing. This applies to soccer, too. On every kick, keep your head down and your eyes on the ball as your foot swings through.

If soccer-style kicking is new to you, practice with a stationary ball. Later, you can try kicks with balls coming toward you or moving away from you.

The Instep Kick   A football player, in trying for the extra point after a touchdown or a field goal, kicks with his toe. A soccer player almost never does. The kick that is fundamental to the game is the instep kick. Don't confuse the instep with the inside of the foot. The instep is the arched upper surface of the foot, the part beneath the lacing of your shoe. Kicking with the instep, since it puts a wide surface of the foot in contact with the ball, helps you to achieve accuracy when you pass and shoot. It also produces kicks that send the ball great distances.

To execute an instep kick, stride forward and plant your non-kicking foot alongside the ball, with your toes pointed toward your target. Keep your head down, your eyes on the ball. Let your arms hang loosely at your sides. Swing your kicking leg forward, keeping the knee bent and the toes pointed down and

In the instep kick, the foot should come toward the ball in this fashion.

slightly inward. Straighten the leg as you swing it through. Strike slightly below the center of the ball with the lacing of your shoe. Follow through. The ball will go toward the direction the toe is pointed at the completion of the follow-through. Don't raise your head until the ball is on its way.

Some young players have trouble with this kick because they are in a poor position when the kicking foot makes contact. Bear in mind that the lower leg

(left) Snap the lower leg through after the knee comes over the ball. (right) Really follow through.

should not snap through until the knee is over the ball. The non-kicking leg should be comfortably bent at the knee.

Another difficulty is the fear of stubbing the foot. This can be a painful experience. Begin slowly, striking the ball softly. Even shadow-kick, that is, practice the instep kick without any ball. Remember, power and distance aren't nearly as important as precision.

27

As you become experienced, you'll learn how to vary the trajectory of your kicks by the manner in which you bring your instep into the ball. As a general rule, you'll want to keep the ball low because it then travels with the greatest speed, but occasionally a situation will arise that calls for a lofted shot. To send the ball high, plant your non-kicking foot to the side of the ball and slightly in back of it. When you swing your kicking foot forward, make contact beneath the ball. The instep is then able to impart lift while powering the ball forward as well.

One coach I know teaches the instep kick by having his players don sneakers during practice sessions. This forces the person kicking to use his instep. It's too hard on the toes to do otherwise.

The Inside-of-the-Foot Kick   To be precise, the inside of the foot is the region between the big toe and the point of the anklebone. When you use the inside of the foot to kick, you're likely to get even more accuracy than when you use the instep. This is an excellent method for the short kicks necessary in passing and dribbling, and forward line players find it ideal for shooting when up close; however, it does not give great power or distance.

To execute an inside-of-the-foot kick, stride toward the ball and plant your non-kicking foot to the side and slightly behind the ball. When you swing your kicking foot forward, the knee and foot should be turned outward slightly, and the knee should be bent. Your head must be down, your eyes on the

28

(left) Position for inside-of-the-foot kick. (right) Swing foot forward, keeping knee bent and foot turned slightly outward.

ball. Straighten the leg as you snap it forward. After contact, follow through.

The Outside-of-the-Foot Kick   During a game, you may also use a kick delivered from the outside of your foot. Lift your kicking foot slightly off the ground, and tap the ball with the outside of the foot just behind the small toe. This method is employed for soft flick passes between players on the run.

29

Correct approach for the toe kick

The Toe Kick   Sometimes a fullback will use a toe kick to clear the ball, but it's seldom employed by forwards or halfbacks. It's executed by bringing the toe in direct contact with a ball. While it gives great velocity to the ball, the toe kick isn't nearly as important as the instep kick or the kick delivered from the inside of the foot. These are your basic weapons.

The Volley Kick   The term *volley* is used to describe a type of kick; it's not another method of kicking. You execute a volley anytime you kick the ball before it bounces on the ground. Usually it's an instep kick.

The volley is somewhat difficult to master because you have so little time to judge the speed of the ball, its trajectory, and then to position yourself and kick. Don't concern yourself with the volley kick until you're adept at kicking a stationary ball and a rolling ball.

In competition, the volley kick is used by every player, but it's the particular specialty of the fullbacks. They use it to clear the ball over the head of an oncoming opponent.

There are countless ways to execute the volley kick, depending upon the height of the ball, its speed, and its direction. In cases where the ball comes directly toward you, about knee high, lean back slightly as you move to kick. The ball should be hit just as your leg starts to swing up. Keep the knee of your kicking leg forward of the foot as the leg swings through. Your arms will feel most comfortable and give better balance if they are out to your sides. The farther back you lean, the higher the ball will go.

The volley is almost always an instep kick.

Variations of the volley kick include the overhead volley, wherein the kick is executed above the level of the head, an acrobatic maneuver, as you can judge. There is also the hook volley, one executed from an oblique, or leaning, approach.

The Half Volley   Kicking the ball just as it rebounds off the ground is known as a half volley. It's an instep kick, but one that requires a keen sense of timing. Kick too early or too late and it's sure to go awry.

To execute a half volley, keep your body well over the ball. Don't bring your kicking leg through until the knee is over the ball—just as in the conventional instep kick. Keep your head down. Follow through. When properly performed, the half volley kick will zoom the ball far downfield.

PASSING   Success in modern soccer depends on teamwork, and the essence of teamwork is the pass, the transfer of the ball from one player to another. Fast, accurate passes are what spark offensive play, while listless, poorly directed passes are certain to strain any team's attack.

A pass can be delivered with the foot, the leg, the chest, or any other part of the body except the arms. Passes can be long or short; indeed, every time you kick the ball, except when you're shooting, it is a pass.

Most passes are the result of inside-of-the-foot kicks (page 28). Sometimes you only have to push

32

the ball; other times you'll really want to power it. In either case, your body should be almost over the ball, and your foot only a few inches from the ground.

When the ball comes to you high off the ground, you'll probably want to use a volley kick (page 30) to pass. Use the inside of your foot, however. This type of pass, since it soars high in the air, is sometimes referred to as a *lob*. It requires plenty of knee action.

Use the instep kick (page 25) for long passes. You can also pass using the outside of your foot, the sole, or the heel. Use the outside of the foot just in back of the little toe to get off short passes. This should be an abrupt movement with little follow-through.

Using the sole of the foot is the accepted way

Use the sole of your foot to pass backward.

of passing backward. This pass must be performed while the ball is stationary. Simply place your foot on the ball and roll it backward. The motion is the same as when you're wiping the sole of your shoe on a mat.

You can also pass backward by using the back of your heel. Step over the ball, then punch it back. Of course, the heel pass and the sole-of-the-foot pass are only effective in short-range situations.

The paragraphs above explain some of the different ways to execute passes, but the art is not as simple as these instructions may imply. Passing has

You can also execute a back pass by punching the ball with the back of your heel.

A pass should lead the receiver so that he can gather it in without breaking stride.

a high degree of subtlety to it. Never let your actions reveal precisely when or to where you are going to pass. Try to mask your intentions for as long as possible.

Don't ever pass blindly. Know where your teammates are positioned. When you send the ball on its way, "lead" the receiver so that he can gather it in without breaking stride. This means you should know the capabilities of each one of your teammates. Some will be able to take a long lead; others will require that the ball be directed almost to their feet. After passing, always get in position for a return pass.

The power of the pass should fit the situation. If the receiver is near you, you may only have to nudge the ball. A ball with too much speed can be difficult to handle and lead to an interception.

Keep in mind that the longer the pass, the greater the chance that it will be intercepted. Shorten your range if your passes aren't getting to their intended receivers.

All players should be skilled in the "wall pass," wherein you use a teammate as if he were a sturdy upright structure. The tactic is used when you're about to come under attack. Quickly send the ball to your teammate. Skim past the tackler and then receive a pass back—off the "wall."

A specialized passing strategy is required when you're in the penalty area. Avoid playing the ball from one side of the field to the other. Instead, work to penetrate. For a winger, this may mean picking out a player and booting him a short, decisive pass as he moves in.

Unfortunately, most American players, and many English players also, don't emphasize the pass enough. Practice sessions are often largely devoted to kicking, trapping, and taking shots at the goal, es-

36

pecially the last named. But passing deserves more practice than any other aspect of your game. Practice with a partner. Pass the ball back and forth while running up and down the field. Begin with simple inside-of-the-foot passes. Practice long instep passes. Pass off your chest and head. Always concentrate on moving the ball fast and accurately.

TRAPPING   When you trap the ball, you "kill" it —stop it—and get it in position to dribble, pass, or shoot. You can use any part of your body to trap except your arms and hands.

Be relaxed and well balanced when you're preparing to trap, and always "give" a little when the ball makes contact. This applies whether you are trapping with your foot, body, or head, and whether the ball is rolling, bouncing, or traveling very fast. When you "ride" with the ball, you absorb its impact and prevent it from bounding away. It's similar to the way a catcher gloves a pitcher's fastball. He pulls his hand back slightly as the ball thumps into the mitt. You utilize the same principle in stopping the soccer ball dead. And, of course, always keep your eyes on the ball.

Trapping with the Foot   Use the inside of your foot to trap a rolling ball or one that comes in low. Follow the ball closely. Lean toward it. Lift the sole of your trap foot from the ground, and use the inside of the foot as a wedge to stifle the ball's roll against the ground.

Trapping: (left) with inside of foot, (right) with sole

Use the sole of your foot, too. But be wary. If an opponent is moving in to tackle, you could be setting up the ball for him.

You can also use the outside of your foot to trap a ball that's rolling toward you, although it is a difficult art. Allow the ball to pass in front of your body, then cross the trapping leg in front of the other leg, wedging the ball between the outside of the foot and the ground. With this method, a player is usually in perfect position to recover, then pass or shoot.

To trap a ball that comes in on a bounce, again use the inside of your foot. Timing is all important, but the same principle applies: smother the ball between the inside of your foot and the ground.

38

Trapping a ball in midair with the instep

Foreign players display incredible skill with their feet when trapping the ball. Watching them can be a valuable lesson. Many can literally catch the ball in midair on an instep, and then bring the ball to the ground in perfect position for a pass or a shot at the goal. It takes remarkable feel to be able to do this.

Trapping with the Leg   Use one shin or both of them to snare balls that bounce right in front of you. Keep your legs slightly apart. Bend your knees; lift your heels from the ground. As the ball rebounds, sink lower, trapping the ball within the angle formed by your shins and the ground.

When a ball comes in waist high, either on the bounce or airborne, you can trap it with the inside

Trapping with the leg

of the thigh. Hold the trapping leg as if you were about to step up a stair—the knee well bent, the foot off the ground. Face the inside of the thigh toward the ball. Rotate the thigh outward slightly to cushion the impact. Don't try the thigh trap in competition unless you've practiced it faithfully. If your timing isn't faultless, you can miss the ball completely.

40

Trapping with the Upper Body The chest offers a broad, easily controlled surface on which to trap the ball. In the case of a ball that soars to you in the air, lean back. When the ball strikes your chest, rise up on your toes and draw your stomach in to deaden the impact. The ball should drop to the ground in front of your feet.

Trap the ball on your chest, and then carom it downward.

41

When the ball bounces to you, lean forward from the waist. The idea is to carom the ball from your chest downward.

Remember to keep your hands away from your body when you're chesting the ball. Stretch them outward. This helps your balance and avoids interference with the trap.

Many professional players display sheer artistry when using the chest to trap. Pelé, in fact every member of the Santos of Brazil squad, has the ability to only slightly deaden the ball when it strikes, deflecting it behind defending players so as to create openings for goalward spurts. The Brazilians, as well as most other top-ranked players, can pass accurately using the chest, and Alan Gilzean, one of Scotland's foremost players, is accomplished in turning either right or left while the ball rides on his chest, thus setting himself up for a pass or a shot.

You can also use the stomach to trap the ball, although its use is usually limited to balls that come in on a bounce. With arms out to the sides, lean forward as the ball nears. Deflect it downward.

Trapping the ball with the head—the forehead, to be specific—is an art very few players ever master. To be able to deaden the ball as it strikes involves relaxing the neck muscles at precisely the right instant. Then you dip down on one knee. Only the cleverest of professional soccer players or jugglers can do it. The better way of handling a ball that comes in high is to head it.

42

HEADING   Heading the ball is just what the phrase implies—striking it with your head. Does it hurt? Not if you do it correctly.

It's important to strike the ball with the front part of your forehead, just below the hairline. This is the sturdiest part of the skull. In addition, this method enables your eyes to follow the flight of the oncoming ball right up until the last second.

If you are somewhat fearful about heading, practice with a ball that's soft or a balloon. Once you've learned to use your head properly, you won't experience any pain, even with a fully inflated ball. Practice with a partner. Have him toss the ball to you, and you head it back. It must come in at least chin high. Or

When you head, strike the ball with the front part of your forehead.

you can suspend the ball from an overhead branch or crossbar. In any case, begin heading from a standing-still position.

Face the oncoming ball squarely. Sink in the knees, and tilt your head back, and your shoulders and upper torso as well. Just before contact, lunge into the ball—straighten your knees, snap your head and upper torso forward. Really punch into the ball; don't let it merely drop onto your head. Follow through with your head in the direction you want the ball to go.

(left) Sink in your knees as you go to head. (right) Then lunge for the ball.

Watch the ball carefully as it comes toward you. Don't close your eyes as the ball comes near, although this is likely to mean you'll have to overcome the natural tendency to shut them.

Another fault the beginning soccer player sometimes displays is the tendency to pull in his neck turtlelike at the moment of contact. The right way, of course, is to extend the neck at impact. This enables the strong muscles of the neck to power the ball on its way.

Once you've become skilled in executing a header forward from a standing-still position, you can try some variations. Learn to head the ball forward and back, and on the run and while jumping. You may be surprised at the height and distance the ball travels the first time you jump and head.

To execute a jumping header, face into the oncoming ball squarely. Keep your eyes glued to it. Drive off on one foot without breaking stride. Keep your head and upper torso tilted back. Snap the head forward as you make contact. The neck muscles will absorb the shock of impact.

Be mindful of your arms when you jump to head. Use your arms to maintain your balance. Be careful not to wave them heedlessly for you're likely to cause a foul, especially if you're surrounded by players.

Heading the ball is not a natural skill like running or throwing, but anyone who practices can become accomplished. The knowledge of how to head is

Professional players execute jumping headers.

absolutely vital to modern soccer play. Halfbacks and
fullbacks head the ball when clearing corner kicks.
And the head is a perfect way to pass at short range;
it's quicker than a kick. Last, you can use the heading
maneuver to score. Little wonder that soccer players
refer to the art as "kicking with the head."

46

TACKLING   In soccer the tackle is a blocking or interfering maneuver used to take the ball away from an opposing player. Unlike football, wherein a tackle involves seizing a player and throwing him to the ground, the action of the soccer tackle is focused upon the ball. It is a swift and daring maneuver, as opposed to one that is essentially violent.

Gaining control of the ball is not the only motive of the tackle. With a well-executed tackle, you can force an opponent to send the ball out of bounds, giving your team possession. Tackling can also cause your opponent to make a bad pass. It's easy to understand why tackling is so extremely important. All players must know how to tackle, and halfbacks and fullbacks must be virtuoso performers.

One secret to success in tackling is knowing precisely when to make your move. If the man with the ball is advancing it with just one foot, then on every other stride the ball is going to be out of his immediate control.

You can tackle from the front, the side, or from the rear. The front tackle is the simplest of the three. The idea is to loom up in front of the opposing player, blocking his forward progress. Remember, you can use your shoulders to block the dribbler, but pushing with your hands or elbows is not allowed.

For a front tackle, first block the ball with one foot; and then quickly flick it away with the other foot toward the dribbler's weak side). Get your body between the ball and the dribbler, with your right shoulder opposite his right shoulder. It's vital that you crouch slightly so that the collision won't throw you off balance, and try to keep your body weight well over the ball. Once you've wrested the ball from the dribbler's control, fire a pass to a teammate; or, if you're in a hazardous position near your goal, clear the ball upfield.

When you tackle from the side, the basic technique is the same. Run alongside the dribbler, shoulder him, then kick the ball away. There's no need to get your body between the ball and the dribbler. It's more of a steal.

Tackling from the side may mean that you will slide into the ball along the ground, trying to grab the ball away with your foot. Sometimes this is called a hook tackle. Beware; this can cause injury. Tackling from the rear is also hazardous and should be

A perfectly executed front tackle. The ball is quickly flicked aside and passed to a teammate or sent upfield.

*(left) A side tackle (right) A rear tackle, a hazardous maneuver
that should be attempted only by very experienced players*

left to players of long experience.

Bear in mind that you should always be somewhat cautious about tackling. Before you move in, be sure you're aware of how your teammates are positioned. Don't allow a missed tackle to leave your team vulnerable.

The dribbler has the advantage. He knows where he is going with the ball and what moves he is going to make, and you do not. Thus, you may be deceived

49

by a feint and made to look ridiculous. You can help to prevent this by keeping your eyes on the ball. Don't be distracted by the dribbler's hips, legs, or feet.

Often, of course, the playing situation dictates whether or not you should launch a tackle. You should never hesitate about attacking an opponent who has the ball in front of the penalty area. When he is in his own territory, he is not as much of a threat.

Not every player is strong enough or daring enough to be a successful tackler. But while a player may not be physically suited to challenging a dribbler and taking possession of the ball, he should at least be skilled in putting up resistance and forcing the opposition into errant passes.

THROWING-IN One expert has estimated that throw-in plays take up about fifteen per cent of the playing time in any given game. Thus, the throw-in deserves special attention. Every player should be accomplished in the art.

There's nothing difficult about the throw-in. Simply grasp the ball in both hands, spreading your fingers comfortably apart. Your hold should be slightly to the rear of the ball, since the idea is to fling it through the air in much the same fashion a stone is cast from a slingshot. Place the ball well behind your head. Position your left foot about a stride ahead of your right. (The rules state that both feet must be on or in back of the sideline.) You get power into the throw by shifting your weight from the rear leg to the

The throw-in. Note how the weight shifts from the rear to the front foot.

front leg. Sink in the knees slightly. Lean back from the waist.

To fire, straighten up and whip the ball away. Rise up on your toes as your weight shifts forward. Follow through with your arms.

Practice this method of throwing until you're accurate, even over long distances. Throw against a wall. As you practice, gradually increase your distance from the wall. This is a good way to develop the muscles used in performing the throw-in.

RUNNING   While kicking, dribbling, trapping, and tackling are the acknowledged fundamentals of the game, don't overlook the importance of running and knowing how to run. Whenever you are in a soccer game, you will spend approximately three-quarters of your time running as you seek to get in position for a pass, a shot, or to defend.

Watch the way a top-notch soccer player runs. He's always on his toes, alert to move in any direction. Try to develop this habit.

Use short strides and keep your body erect. This will make it easier for you to start, stop, and shift direction. For balance, keep your arms wide of your body. When you're not running, you should at least be jogging, alert to dart into position.

CHAPTER FOUR

THE POSITIONS

Soccer is played with eleven men on a team. They are usually a goalkeeper, two fullbacks, three halfbacks, and five forwards. This chapter explains the specific duties that relate to each assignment.

If there is one characteristic that applies to every position, it is versatility. Modern soccer is a fast, fluid game, with the possession of the ball constantly shifting from one team to another. A player who is attacking one minute will be defending the next, and this means that individuals must be able to move quickly and easily from one set of duties to another. Every outstanding player in the game displays this quality.

What position should you play? To a great extent the answer depends upon how fast you are. If you can flash up and down the field with the ball faster than anyone else in your group, then you'll probably do best as a forward. If you have about average speed, you should consider becoming a halfback. If you want a position that will not necessarily demand speed, you might try for the fullback spot. Of course, I don't

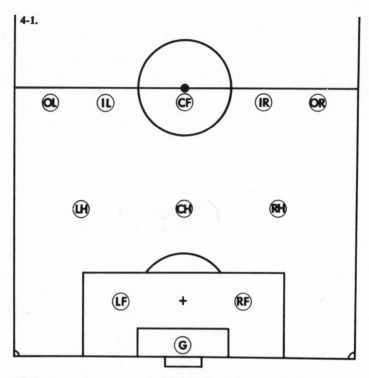

Players on each team are arranged in this fashion at the start of the game. (OL-outside left, IL-inside left, CF-center forward, IR-inside right, OR-outside right, LH-left halfback, CH-center halfback, RH-right halfback, LF-left fullback, RF-right fullback, G-goalkeeper)

mean to imply that speed is the only skill you require to become a soccer player. Not at all. But time and time again I've seen speed prove a dependable criterion for choosing a position.

FULLBACKS The fullbacks' chief responsibilities are defensive, with the rival outside forwards their foremost concern, but they also occasionally cover

54

the opposing center halfback. As this suggests, the fullbacks must be adept at taking the ball away from enemy players. They must be gifted in kicking and heading, skills necessary to get rid of the ball quickly.

In days past, the fullback was noted for his strength and brawn. But not anymore. Nowadays the fullback must often think like a forward and act like one. All are agile and some are extremely fast.

The fullback must have the ability to get good distance with his kicks, sending the ball from deep within his own territory across midfield to an open teammate. Such kicks have to be directed with great care. A kick without purpose is likely to serve as the launching pad for an enemy strike. The fullback should target on an open forward or one of his half-backs.

The fullback rarely dribbles the ball, and only rarely does he get into the opposition side of the field. He has to be particularly skilled in getting rid of the ball. This is easy to understand. His duties keep him deep inside his own territory and, thus, should he be tackled and beaten, the result can be a severly weakened line of defense.

It takes courage to be a fullback. Sometimes he has to charge headlong to thwart an enemy who is pouring in on the goal. Often his body becomes the target for enemy shooters.

"Play the man outside" is what coaches tell their fullbacks. In other words, force the opposition players to the sidelines. Then, when an enemy player does unload a goalward kick, his target area is relatively small. The greatest hazard is to have a player shoot from the middle of the field, from head on, that is.

Fullbacks, in defending against opposition forwards, have to be a bit cautious about tackling. Sometimes the tackler is wise to force the dribbler out of bounds or allow him to pass. After all, the fullback is the only remaining line of defense before the goalkeeper. When he's beaten on a tackle, and there's no backup man, the goalkeeper will be in a more vulnerable position.

Fullbacks, from midget league players to international stars, must cope with the two-on-one situation—two forwards, working in combination, who drive in on a lone fullback. Caution should be the keynote here. The fullback must resist the urge to go for the ball. Instead, he should retreat before the attack, being certain to keep his body between the ball and the goal. The idea is to slow down the action until help arrives.

In cases where there is no support, the fullback's main concern should be the man who does not have the ball, not the dribbler. It's the assist man who is likely to get the pass off which the score-attempting shot will be taken.

In all cases the fullback has to be careful not to retreat so deep that he blocks the goalkeeper's view of the ball. Whenever the goalie leaves his post to pursue the ball, one of the fullbacks should slide into the goal as replacement.

HALFBACKS The greater part of any soccer game takes place between a team's penalty area and the midfield stripe, and this is generally where the halfbacks roam. Thus, halfbacks play key roles on both offense and defense. It is often said that a team with three competent halfbacks on the field will be in control of the ball much of the time.

Specifically, halfbacks have three essential duties: they defend against enemy forwards; they provide a link between their own forwards and the deep defensive players; and they support their own forwards when on the attack.

Halfbacks must be quick and strong and, since they usually do more running than the other players, they must have endurance. In addition, they must be gifted playmakers and sure defenders.

The game situation and playing characteristics of their opponents determine how the halfbacks position themselves on the field, but it's usual for one of the outside, or wing, halfbacks to penetrate deep into the opponent's territory, supporting the play of the related outside forward. The other outside halfback remains back, alert to intercept passes and otherwise support the defense. The center halfback stations himself in between the two outside backs. Of course, there is great flexibility in these assignments as play moves up and down the field.

Sometimes the outside halfbacks are responsible for defending against the rival outside forwards. The fullbacks then have the responsibility to cover the opposing inside forwards. In other cases, the outside halfbacks take the inside forwards. As this implies, there must be the closest of working relationships between the halfbacks and fullbacks. They sometimes switch defensive assignments during a game in their attempt to bewilder the opposition.

Suppose a halfback is covering an inside forward. If his man gets the ball, the halfback's duty is to tackle quick and hard. Then he must get the ball to a forward who can lead a scoring threat. Last, the halfback trails the play to assist. It's unusual to see a halfback dribble. If he does, it's simply to draw an enemy player out of position. Halfbacks rely on quick, accurate passes to move the ball.

The center half, because of his strategic location, is often a key figure on both defense and offense. He should be taller than average, and be able to leap high in the air and head the ball.

Frequently his principal assignment is to shadow the opposing center forward. Thus, he often covers more territory than any of the other backs. He must be able to tackle, trap, and pass; and, more than anyone else, he must be accomplished in "reading" the game situation, anticipating enemy strategy. Aggressiveness is another quality the center half must boast. If the situation demands, he should not hesitate about charging the center forward.

FORWARDS The forwards are the principal striking force of a team. The five-man forward line is made

58

up of one center forward, two inside forwards (one left and one right), and two outside forwards (one left and one right). Sometimes the outside forwards are termed *wings* or *wingers*.

All players in the forward line must be well qualified in kicking, trapping, passing, heading, and dribbling. They must be accurate when shooting and know how to feint. If you are a forward, study the opposition carefully. Look for the weak spots and build your scoring plays accordingly. Make your passes count. Short, quick passes are the most difficult to intercept, but remember to vary your attack by mixing them with long passes. Whenever you are in range, be ready to shoot.

The center forward, because of his central position on the attacking line, is invariably the team's chief scoring threat. Often he is called a *striker*. The center forward, along with the inside forwards, keynotes his team's playmaking and the scoring forays that penetrate deep into enemy territory.

A center forward must be extremely mobile. He has to be able to kick skillfully with either foot, pass in any direction, and be a master dribbler. He must be a gifted header. As for his speed, he is often the fastest man on the team. Of course, he has to be able to shoot hard and accurately.

Yet despite all of his individual talents, the center forward is no loner. His skills must always blend with those of his teammates. Since he is usually guarded closely, he serves as an excellent decoy,

The goalkeeper reaches out to intercept the ball when the center forward tries for a goal.

luring defensemen out of position to create an opening for an inside forward to dash goalward.

But it is for his ability to put the ball in the net that the center forward is often most noted. This means he must always be in a position for a pass. And he must so station himself that when he does receive the ball, he can pour in for a shot or work in combination with one of his teammates to create a scoring thrust. On defense, the center forward seldom goes deeper than the far edge of the center circle.

On a corner kick, the center forward should station himself five to six feet in from the goalmouth, alert to drive the kick into the goal on a rebound or by means of a head. On a throw-in, he should position himself within range of the man throwing in.

Because he is often the best shot on the team, the center forward is usually entrusted to take penalty kicks. He should work on these during practice sessions. If he is not doing the kicking, he should position himself at the front line of the penalty area, alert to play a rebound.

The center forward should have a knowledge of defensive play, but this is quite secondary to him. Usually he limits himself to the harassment of the opposing center half or troublesome fullbacks.

Like the center forward, the inside right and inside left forwards must be accomplished passers and playmakers and dependable scorers as well. But unlike the center forward, they often go downfield to help when the defense is under pressure.

The inside forwards are often a link between the outside forwards and the backs. Because of their role as playmakers, and because of their responsibility in assisting on defense, the inside forwards usually cover more ground than any of the other players. They rove. This means they must have great speed and stamina.

On defense, the inside forwards cover the opposing halfbacks. Sometimes an inside forward will devote himself defensively to the center half, usually the most skilled of the backs.

The outside forwards, or wingers, are responsible for patrolling the outside lines of the field. With his team in possession, an outside forward will attempt to bring the ball down his side of the field to the corner. When the defense moves to thwart this maneuver, he sends a crossing or centering pass to a forward who is in position for a scoring thrust.

Besides having good speed, the outside forward must be efficient at controlling the ball, able to trap quickly and pass off. He must be elusive enough to evade the harassment of the halfbacks.

He is often the one who sparks the attack. After a save, the goalie usually fires to a wing, who roars with the ball into the opponent's territory. On a throw-in, it is usually the outside forward who receives the ball. In such cases, he must be careful not to play too close to the sideline because it cuts down his room to maneuver. In recent years, there has been a growing tendency for the outside forward to leave his post near the sideline to switch positions with an inside forward, the center forward, or even a halfback in his efforts to elude a defender.

Corner kicks are usually taken by the outside forwards. Each should work to develop a kick that plunks down six to eight yards in front of the goalmouth.

On defense, the outside forwards assist the fullbacks. Usually they cover the wingers, freeing the fullbacks to take positions near the goal. Seldom do they penetrate as deep into enemy territory as do their inside counterparts.

GOALKEEPER For backs and forwards, soccer is a game of running, passing, and constant shifting between offense and defense. For goalkeepers, the game is much different. Goalkeepers seldom run; they never dribble. They are the only players who are allowed to use their hands on the ball. Obviously, playing goalie is very much of a specialty, requiring the knowledge of a distinct set of fundamentals.

Even those with only the slightest knowledge of soccer realize that the goalkeeper's chief responsibility is to prevent the ball from entering his team's goal. But in modern soccer the goalie is also expected to trigger his team's attack with well-aimed passes— either throwing or kicking the ball—to open receivers.

What qualities make an efficient goalie? Good eyesight is a must. Greater-than-average height and reach are other plus factors. A goalie must have strong arms, shoulders, and legs and sure hands. He has to be agile, able to move quickly and nimbly from one side to the other. He has to have the ability to concentrate, even when the play is on the opposite end of the field. Finally, he must always be a cool performer, maintaining his skill and confidence in the face of the furious play that sometimes envelops the goalmouth. This is clearly a demanding position.

The best way to stop the ball is to catch it. But don't reach or dive for the ball unless absolutely necessary. Try to get your body behind the ball. In this way, you can use your upper body and your legs to stifle the force of the shot.

This means you must take a well-balanced stance, one that enables you to move either right or left with equal facility. Bend your knees slightly. Relax. Position yourself about a foot in front of the goal line. When you must move, sidestep.

The goalie's stance is relaxed and well balanced.

When a ball comes in hugging the ground, move in front of it and get down on one knee or squat. Field it in the same way a baseball infielder handles a "grass cutter." If you're unable to collar it with your hands, block it with your chest or shoulders.

Shots that come toward you at waist level are a bit easier to handle. With arms outstretched get in front of the ball; catch it, and then allow your stomach to absorb the force of the impact.

Of course, it's not always possible for you to get your body in front of the ball. High shots are the best example of this. In such cases, spring into the air, and, using the fingers of both hands, deftly tip the ball up and over the crossbar. Never try for a catch if the ball seems headed beyond your reach. Deflecting it is the safest policy. As one goalie has observed, "Never be afraid to put the ball into the crowd. There's no one there who can score against you." When the ball is close to one of the posts, you may have to dive to make a save, attempting to tip it with your fingers around the upright.

An experienced goalie will sometimes "fist" the ball—punch it with the knuckles or side of the fist— to a teammate. Usually this tactic is reserved for balls that come in high. But controlling the ball with one fist or even both of them is difficult. A tip is almost always the better course of action.

One thing you must never do as a goalkeeper is attempt to kick the ball while defending. The ball is

High shots should be deflected over the goal.

very likely to bound over your foot or deflect crazily from your leg into the goal. Always go for the ball with your hands. Get possession!

Once you do get possession of the ball, get rid of it as fast as you can. Throw it to a teammate. Don't lob it. Really throw. It should be similar to the way in

A rapid-fire throw gets rid of the ball.

which an outfielder pegs to second base to get a
runner trying to stretch a base hit. Get your body into
the throw. Follow through, pointing your hand in the
direction you want the ball to go. You are usually wise
to throw diagonally to the left or right rather than
straight down the middle. And, if possible, throw to

the flank opposite to the direction from which the ball has come. There is likely to be less traffic for your teammates on that side.

Sometimes it's advantageous to roll the ball to a teammate. Just be certain there are no opponents close. And when you want to clear the ball far down-

Sometimes it's best to roll the ball to a teammate.

A clearing kick gets the ball downfield.

field, a kick may be the wisest strategy. Punt the ball like a football player. Use your instep and really put power behind the kick, but be sure to target on one of your teammates.

Watch out for rebounds off the posts. Get out and cover them quickly. Never allow an attacker a follow-up shot.

Perhaps the most ticklish aspect of the goalkeeper's job is knowing when to leave the goal to go out and meet an attacker. Suppose the center forward has eluded the fullbacks and is heading in like an express train. As the goalkeeper, you're a sitting duck. In such cases, the best defense is a strong attack.

Leave the goal; swoop toward the attacker, seeking either to gain possession or force a wild shot.

The judgment whether to go out or stay in the goal has to be made in the blink of an eye. And once you decide to meet the oncoming player, move like lightning. Don't delay an instant. Remember, help is on the way and you only have to delay his shot for a few seconds. But you can't go out too early. The result can be calamitous. The attacker can lob the ball over your head into the net, or, if he's skilled enough, dribble around you and still have a wide angle for a shot. You'll learn from experience.

Penalty kicks from the penalty spot deserve special mention. In such cases, don't try to outguess the kicker. Depend upon your reflexes and the knowledge that the kicker will be aiming for a target close to one of the posts. Position yourself in the center of the goal, your feet on the goal line. As soon as the kicker commits himself, dive—make your play. On corner kicks, move out a foot or two from the goal line and face the kicker. Move any teammate who is blocking your view of the ball.

Much of goalkeeping is reflexive, and you'll find yourself moving naturally from post to post as you position yourself to block shots. You can improve your advantage by studying the playing characteristics of the enemy. Does the center forward fire without first trapping? Is he adept at shooting with his left foot as well as his right? Do the halfbacks shoot or do they prefer to feed the forwards? How do the halfbacks

A goalie makes a diving save.

feed—do they try to slice the ball between opposing backs, or do they pass for a spot? Answers to questions like these will provide you with information that will make your job a great deal easier.

You should also know the strengths and weaknesses of the members of your own team. Who are the individuals that are best able to handle a stinging pass? Who are the ones that are sometimes guilty of defensive lapses?

On many teams the goalkeeper is the field general, holding a status somewhat similar to the catcher in baseball or the quarterback in football. When play comes close, he shouts warnings and defensive instructions to his teammates. He's the chief morale builder.

Goalkeepers are more likely to be victimized by weather and adverse conditions than any other player on the field. A wet ball is much more difficult to hold, you need a firmer grip. Get a good idea of wind conditions before the game begins. A high kick into the wind can sail erratically, first climbing like a frightened bird, then plummeting down. Crosswinds also have a weird effect upon the ball.

Remember, as your team's goalie, you are the last line of defense. Many a time the outcome of the game is going to depend on your skill more than anyone else's. Keep those skills in razor-sharp condition by constant practice.

CHAPTER FIVE

SOCCER RULES

While the origin of soccer is shrouded in the mists of the past, the rules of the game are known to date to 1862, the year J. C. Thring wrote down ten basic rules, probably based on the games played at Cambridge, England. In 1863 the English Football Association established a set of seventeen "laws" for players to follow. Surprisingly, in the more than one hundred years that have passed very few changes have been made. Soccer has always been a very simple game and apparently it always will be.

The official rule book of soccer, as published by the United States Soccer Football Association, is a mere sixteen-page pamphlet. If you would like a copy, write the U.S.S.F.A., Empire State Building, Room 4010, New York City, N.Y., 10001. The booklet costs 25 cents. What follows is a condensation and explanation of the rules it contains, excluding the rules on equipment, discussed in Chapter Two.

THE FIELD A soccer field is rectangular, and is from 100 to 130 yards in length, and from 50 to 100 yards in width. (In international matches, the length is 110 to 120 yards, and the width 70 to 80 yards. In Amateur Cup play, the length is 105 to 120 yards, and the width 60 to 80 yards.)

The field is divided by a *halfway line*. The center of the field is indicated by a *center mark*. It is enclosed by a circle having a 10-yard radius, which is called the *center circle*.

The *goal area* at each end of the field is drawn at right angles to the goal line at a distance of 6 yards from each goalpost. It is 20 yards in width and extends 6 yards deep into the playing field.

The *penalty area* at each end of the field is drawn at right angles to the goal line at a distance of 18 yards from each goalpost. It is 44 yards in width and 18 yards in length. The *penalty spot* is a mark within the penalty area and 12 yards from the midpoint of the goal line. The *penalty area arc* is the arc of a circle that has the penalty spot as its center and a 10 yard radius; it is drawn outside the penalty area. The *corner area* is a quarter circle with a radius of one yard at each corner of the field. A flag is placed at each corner.

Each goal is 8 feet high and 8 yards wide. A net may be attached to the goalposts and crossbar.

NUMBER OF PLAYERS A team is composed of eleven players, one of whom is the goalkeeper. A player is allowed to switch positions with the goal-

74

THE FIELD

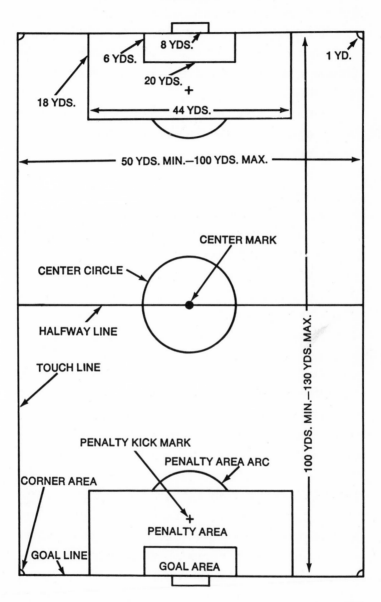

8 YDS.

6 YDS.

1 YD.

20 YDS.

18 YDS.

44 YDS.

50 YDS. MIN.—100 YDS. MAX.

CENTER MARK

CENTER CIRCLE

HALFWAY LINE

TOUCH LINE

100 YDS. MIN.—130 YDS. MAX.

PENALTY KICK MARK

PENALTY AREA ARC

CORNER AREA

PENALTY AREA

GOAL LINE

GOAL AREA

75

keeper during a game, provided the referee is informed in advance of the change.

Two substitutions are allowed in National Open and Amateur Cup games. In other matches, teams usually agree beforehand as to how many substitutes may play.

Once a player is ejected from the game, he is not allowed to return, and his team must play at a numerical disadvantage.

OFFICIALS   A referee officiates each game, enforcing the rules and deciding any disputed point. He can caution or eject players guilty of "misconduct or ungentlemanly behavior." He can stop the game if a player is injured or when rules are broken. He has the power to terminate the game because of bad weather or because of interference on the part of spectators. The referee also serves as the game's timekeeper.

The referee is assisted by two linesmen, who are equipped with small flags. In addition to helping control the game, they indicate when the ball goes out of play and which team is entitled to the corner kick, goal kick, or throw-in. Usually, each linesman is responsible for watching half the field.

DURATION OF THE GAME   A regulation game is 90 minutes in length, divided into 45-minute halves. In National Junior Challenge Cup play and other junior competition, a game is 60 minutes in length, divided into 30-minute halves.

The referee is the chief official at each game.

A half may be extended to permit a penalty kick. In each half, time-outs due to accidents or injuries are to be added to the normal playing time. The half time intermission lasts five minutes, unless more time is granted by the referee.

PLAY OF THE GAME   A coin toss decides which team kicks off. The team that wins the toss has the choice of either kicking off or selecting the side it wishes to defend.

The game starts on a signal from the referee, with a player kicking the ball from the center mark into his opponent's half of the field. Each player must be in his half of the field, and the opposing team must be at least 10 yards from the ball. The ball is not deemed in play "until it has travelled the distance of its own circumference." The kicker cannot play the ball a second time until it has been touched or played by another player. A goal cannot be scored directly from the kickoff.

A similar kickoff play is used after a goal has been scored, with a player representing the team scored against doing the kicking. A kickoff is also used to open the second half; the kicker is a player from the team that received the ball at the opening of the game.

Should the game be temporarily halted, play is restarted by having the referee drop the ball on the spot where it was when play ended. The ball is deemed in play when it touches the ground.

78

The ball is out of play when it crosses the goal line or touchline or whenever the game is halted by the referee. The ball is in play at all other times, even when it rebounds from a goalpost, crossbar, or flag post into the field of play, or rebounds from a referee or linesman.

SCORING   A goal is scored and one point is awarded when the "whole of the ball" passes over the goal line, between the goalposts, and under the cross-bar, provided it has not been thrown, carried, or otherwise propelled by the hand or arm of a player on the attacking team.

The team scoring the greater number of points is the winner. If no goals are scored, or if an equal number of goals are scored by each team, the game is declared a draw.

OFFSIDE   A player is declared offside if he is nearer his opponent's goal line than the ball at the moment the ball is played. A player cannot be ruled offside if he is in his own half of the field, or when there are two opponents nearer to the goal line than he is, or in a case where the ball last touched an opponent or was played by him. There are no offsides on a corner kick, goal kick, throw-in, or when the ball is dropped by the referee.

In the case of an offside infraction, an indirect free kick (page 81) is awarded the opposing team from the spot where the offside occurred.

MISCONDUCT AND FOULS A foul is charged should any player intentionally: a) kick or attempt to kick an opponent; b) trip or attempt to trip an opponent; c) jump an opponent; d) charge "in a violent or dangerous manner;" e) charge an opponent from behind unless the opponent is obstructing; f) strike or attempt to strike an opponent; g) hold an opponent with his hand or arm; h) push an opponent with his hand or arm; i) handle, carry, strike, or otherwise propel the ball with his hand or arm. (This does not apply to goalkeeper when he is within his own penalty area.) The penalty for these infractions is a direct free kick (page 81) awarded to the offended team. It is taken from the spot where the offense occurred.

Should the defensive team commit one of the nine fouls listed above within the penalty area, a penalty kick (page 82) is awarded to the other team.

A foul is also charged to any player who: a) plays in a manner deemed dangerous by the referee; b) charges an opponent with his shoulder when the ball is not within playing distance; c) intentionally obstructs an opponent when not playing the ball; and d) charges the goalkeeper, except when he is holding the ball, obstructing an opponent, or has passed outside his goal area. An indirect free kick is awarded the team offended.

A goalkeeper is charged with a foul when he carries the ball and takes more than four steps without bouncing it. An indirect free kick is awarded the other team.

A player can be "cautioned" by the referee, and no penalty imposed, in the case of minor offenses, such as entering the field of play or rejoining the team after play has begun without having first received a signal of approval from the referee. The game is stopped to allow the referee to impose the caution, then restarted by having the referee drop the ball at the spot where the infraction took place.

If a player persists in infringing the rules, if he shows by word or action that he disagrees with a referee's decision, or is guilty of "ungentlemanly conduct," the referee can caution the player and also award the opposing team an indirect kick.

If a player persists in misconduct after having received a caution, if he uses foul or abusive language, or, in the opinion of the referee, he is guilty of "serious foul play," the offending player can be ejected from the game. Play is halted to impose the penalty, then restarted with an indirect free kick by the opposing team.

FREE KICK   The two types of free kicks are direct and indirect. A direct free kick is one on which a goal may be scored directly. On an indirect free kick, a goal cannot be scored directly; the ball must first touch another player. Both types of kick are taken from the place of the infraction.

When a player is taking a direct or indirect free kick from inside his team's penalty area, all opposing players must remain outside the area and at least 10 yards from the ball. The ball is not in play until it has traveled the distance of its own circumference and has cleared the penalty area. If the ball does not clear the penalty area, it must be rekicked. A goalkeeper, in executing a direct or indirect free kick, must kick the ball from where it rests; he cannot touch it with his hands.

When a player takes a direct or indirect free kick from outside his team's penalty area, all opposing players must be at least 10 yards from the ball, unless they are standing on their own goal line between the goalposts. The ball is considered in play once it has traveled the distance of its own circumference.

In the case of a free kick taken from inside a team's penalty area, if an opposing player moves into the penalty area before the kick is taken, the referee can halt the kick until the rule is obeyed. The referee takes the same action in the case of a free kick outside the penalty area, should an opposing player move to a position closer than 10 yards to the ball.

The ball must be standing still when kicked. The kicker cannot play the ball a second time until it has been touched or played by another player.

PENALTY KICK A penalty kick is a direct free kick awarded to a team when the opposing team has committed a foul within the penalty area. The kick is taken from the penalty mark.

When the kick is taken, all players, with the exception of the kicker and the goalkeeper, must be outside the penalty area and at least ten yards from the penalty mark. The goalkeeper must stand on his own goal line between the goalposts. He cannot move his feet until the ball is kicked.

The kicker must kick the ball forward. He cannot play the ball a second time until it has touched or been played by another player. The ball is in play once it has traveled the distance of its own circumference.

If a player on the defending team infringes the rules, the ball is rekicked. If a player on the attacking team infringes the rules, the kick is disallowed—even if a goal is scored—and the ball is rekicked. If the kicker infringes the rules, the opposing team is awarded an indirect free kick from the spot where the infringement took place.

THROW-IN When a ball goes out of bounds over a sideline, it is thrown-in to play from the spot where it crossed the line. The throw-in is awarded to the opponents of the team that last touched the ball.

To execute a throw-in, the thrower must face the field and throw the ball from behind his head and over it. Both feet must be either on the touchline or on the ground outside it. The thrower cannot play the ball until it has been touched or played by another player. If this rule is infringed, an indirect free kick is awarded the opposing team.

The ball is in play as soon as it enters the field of play. A goal cannot be scored directly from a throw-in. If the ball is thrown improperly, it is to be rethrown by the opposing team.

GOAL KICK When an attacking player is the last to touch the ball before it goes out of bounds across the defending team's goal line, but not between the goalposts, a goal kick is awarded the defending team.

The kick is taken by the goalkeeper. The ball is placed down in that half of the goal area nearest to where it crossed the goal line. The goalkeeper is not allowed to touch the ball before he kicks it. He cannot play the ball a second time until it has been touched or played by another player; if he infringes this rule, an indirect free kick is awarded the opposing team. The kicker must kick the ball beyond the penalty area; otherwise the ball must be rekicked.

A goal cannot be scored directly as the result of a goal kick; it must first touch another player. Players of the opposing team must remain outside the penalty area while the kick is being taken.

CORNER KICK When a defending player is the last to touch the ball before it goes out of bounds over the goal line, then a corner kick is awarded the attacking team to put the ball in play. The ball is kicked from the corner arc closest to where the ball crossed the goal line. A goal may be scored directly from a corner kick.

Opposing players must remain at least 10 yards from the ball while the kick is being taken. The kicker is not allowed to play the ball a second time until it has been touched or played by another player. Should this rule be infringed, the offended team is awarded an indirect free kick.

CHAPTER SIX

TEAM PLAY, OFFENSE , AND DEFENSE

When the rules of soccer were first set down in 1862, they were ten in number. The first and most important rule described how a goal was achieved. "A goal," it said, "is scored whenever the ball is forced through the goal and under the bar, except it be thrown by hand."

Today, the method of scoring is described in Law 10. It is somewhat more detailed than the original rule, but the basic idea has not changed. Opposing players attempt to drive the ball "between the goalposts and under the crossbar."

As this evidence suggests, soccer has always been a simple game to play and understand. Yet the game has seen many significant changes. In soccer's early years, English teams were composed of nine attacking players, one defender, and one goalkeeper. As you can imagine, each game was a frantic affair. Little by little, more and more emphasis was put upon passing, defense, and team play. These are all hallmarks of modern soccer, but the last named is especially important. Watch any well-coached team and you will quickly perceive how the various players mesh together like parts in a smooth-running machine. Eleven individuals, each playing for himself, are of little or no value. To succeed, a soccer team must operate as a unit, with each player using his skills for the general good. This is how games are won.

Alertness is another vital quality. Even a second's letdown can be disastrous. In the 1966 World Cup final match between Great Britain and West Germany, England's captain, Bobby Moore, was fouled and awarded a seemingly harmless free kick from near midfield. For a brief moment, the West German players relaxed. Moore struck. He boomed a soaring kick downfield, and Geoff Hurst poured in from the wing position and easily headed the critical, game-tieing goal past the startled goalie. It proved to be the turning point in England's dramatic win.

OFFENSIVE PLAY   On offense, all soccer teams seek to outthink and outmaneuver their opponents with deep penetrations through passing, dribbling, and long clearing kicks intended to pull defending players out of position. Once the defense has reacted to a thrust, the attackers attempt to send passes to open players who shoot the ball.

To achieve this aim, teams arrange themselves in any one of a number of offensive formations. The trend in recent years has been toward a 4-3-3 attacking formation (Diagram 6–1). This was used with

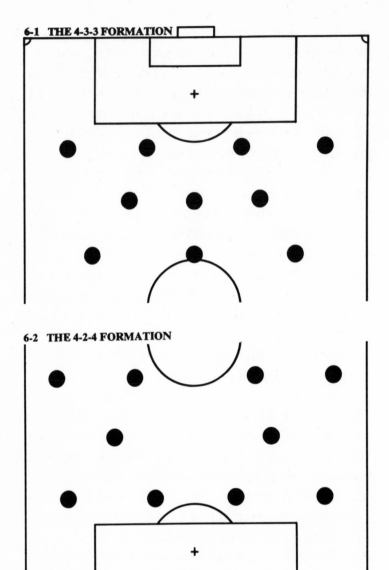

6-1 THE 4-3-3 FORMATION

6-2 THE 4-2-4 FORMATION

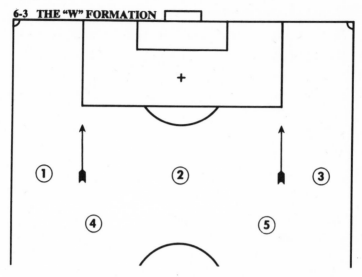

6-3 THE "W" FORMATION

(1-left wing, 2-center forward, 3-right wing, 4-left inside, 5-right inside)

stunning effect by England in 1966 World Cup play. This system employs four backs, three forwards, or strikers, and three midfield players, known as *link men.*

When Brazil won the World Cup in 1958, the team used a 4-2-4 setup (Diagram 6–2). This information utilizes four backs, a forward line composed of two wings and two strikers, and two link men. When on defense, the wing men often drift back to position themselves beside the link men.

Another of soccer's basic attacking formations is the "W." The center and outside forwards are the chief attackers, while the two inside forwards are back (Diagram 6–3). Some teams favor a deep W,

89

with the inside forwards well back; this system stresses the long pass. Other teams play a shallow W, utilizing the short pass.

In this system, the backs work with the forwards by arranging themselves in an "M" setup: the two outside halfbacks are positioned forward of the fullbacks, while the center half pivots back and forth. This so-called W-M formation is popular in every part of the world.

The style of play any given team uses is based to a great extent upon the talents of its players. It also depends on the opposition. Are they a fast team or a slow one? Do they favor short passes or long ones? Are they defensively weaker on one side of the field than the other? Do the individual players dribble too much? Do the fullbacks play side by side or in tandem? Does their goalkeeper have a weak side? Once the answers to these questions and others like them are known, a team can adjust its playing style to take advantage of its opponent's weaknesses and prepare for its strengths. Such preparation will pay rich dividends.

On the opening kickoff, a team can attack in countless ways. It's fundamental, however, to have the outside forwards sweep down the sidelines, then break for the goal, always striving to stay open for a pass. To set up a scoring situation, the center forward can pass off to an inside forward, then race for the goal himself. The inside forward then sends a long pass to the open man (Diagram 6–4).

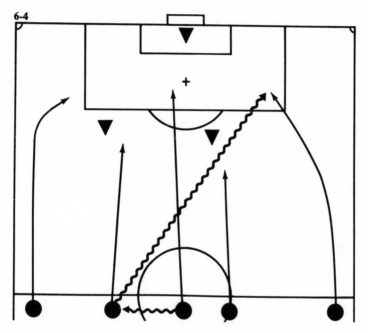

6-4 *On this opening kickoff play, the center forward passes to the inside left forward, then breaks for the goal. The inside left sends a long pass to the outside right. The outside left and the inside right are also streaking goalward.*

A variation of this is to involve a halfback in the play. After receiving a pass from the center forward, the halfback dribbles upfield, giving the streaking forwards additional time to get into position. After drawing a defender, the halfback passes to an open man. (Diagram 6–5). Sometimes on the opening kickoff a team will seek to work the ball goalward with a series of short passes instead of one or two long ones. Diagram 6–6 illustrates.

On the opening kickoff and, indeed, anytime the

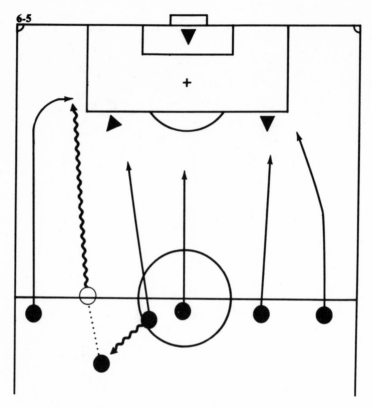

6-5 *This opening kickoff play involves the halfback who takes a pass from the center forward. He dribbles upfield, giving the forwards time to reach the goal area, then passes to an open man, in this case the outside left.*

offense works its way deep into enemy territory, they are at a distinct numerical disadvantage. The number of attacking players is usually seven (five forwards, the center half, and one halfback), as opposed to eleven defensive players. This means attacking players usually have to maneuver to set up a "man-ahead"

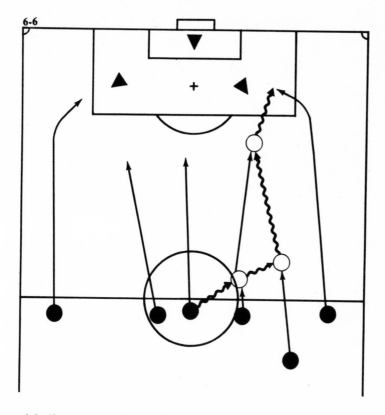

6-6 *Short passes are featured in this opening kickoff play. The ball goes from the center forward, to the inside right, to the right halfback, and then upfield to the inside right a second time. His pass to the outside right results in a scoring attempt.*

situation, that is, a two-on-one or three-on-two situation.

In a two-on-one situation, the two attacking players can elude the lone defender with a simple push pass, with one of the offensive players cutting behind the defender, and toward the goal (Diagram

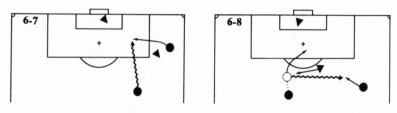

(6-7) *Two offensive players should have little trouble outmaneuvering one defensive player. Here the outside right cuts behind the fullback to take a pass from a teammate.* (6-8) *In this two-on-one situation, the inside left dribbles the ball long enough to draw the defensive player out of position, then passes to the inside right, who is breaking toward the goal. The inside left then cuts toward the goal to receive a possible repass.*

6–7), or with a dribble-pass combination (Diagram 6–8).

The three-on-two situation can be played in a multitude of ways. Just as in the two-on-one, the offensive players can outwit the defense with solely passes or a dribble-pass sequence (Diagram 6–9). Of course, all such plays have to be executed with lightning speed.

These decoy plays are vital not only to free a teammate for a pass, but they are also invaluable in opening up the goal area for a scoring thrust. An offensive player can decoy a defender by simply breaking to the left or right as if to receive a pass (Diagram 6–10), or he can use the ball to decoy (Diagram 6–11).

Besides the various methods of attack outlined above, soccer teams must also be accomplished in playing free kicks—direct or indirect—corner kicks, penalty kicks, goal kicks, and sideline kicks. Teams drill and redrill these situations.

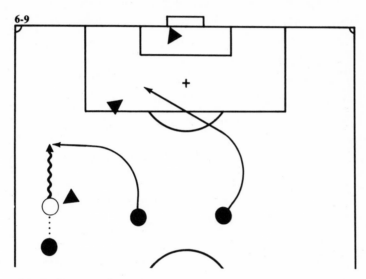

6-9 *In this classic three-on-two situation, a forward dribbles to draw the defender out of position, freeing a teammate for a pass.*

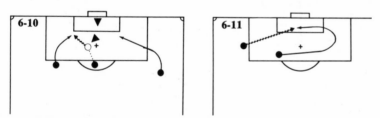

(6-10) *To create a scoring opportunity, first the center forward dribbles toward the goal to draw the fullback out of position. Once this is accomplished, the forward sends a pass to his inside left. The forward then breaks toward the goal for a repass. The inside right also dashes goalward.* **(6-11)** *In this decoy effort, the center forward breaks suddenly to the right. If the fullback follows, the center forward races back for a pass from the left side.*

95

Direct Free Kicks While the rules state that a goal may be scored as a direct result of a free kick, seldom does the defense give the kicker an opportunity for a clear shot. But in clogging up the goal area, they permit a multitude of passing possibilities. When the kick is taken from a point just outside the penalty area, the kicker attempts to send a pass to one of the outside forwards who are breaking for the goal (Diagram 6–12). It may be a push pass or a lob over the heads of the defenders.

In the case where the direct free kick is taken from a point close to the halfway mark, the halfbacks usually become involved in the play (Diagram 6–13). This serves to open up the defense.

6-12

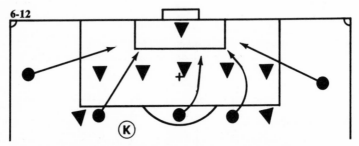

6-12 *In this direct free kick situation, the kicker* (**K**) *can pass to any one of the forwards breaking goalward. Note how the defense has blockaded the goal.*

Indirect Free Kicks Most indirect free kick situations are similar to direct free kicks in both their offensive patterns and defensive alignments, although in most cases the defense does not barricade the goal quite so completely. An indirect free kick can be

96

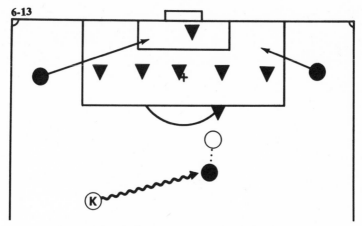

6-13

6-13 *In the direct free kick situation above, the kicker passes to the center halfback, who dribbles upfield. When a defenseman moves to tackle, the halfback sends a lob pass to one of the outside forwards, each of whom is driving toward the goal.*

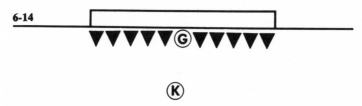

6-14

6-14 *On an indirect kick from a point inside the goal area, the defending players blockade the goal in this fashion.*

taken from a point inside the goal area, and when this occurs the offensive and defensive players have special duties. (When an infraction calling for a direct free kick is incurred within the goal area, the kick is taken from the penalty spot.) The defensive players line up on the goal line between the goal posts (Diagram 6–14). The kicker passes to a forward who

97

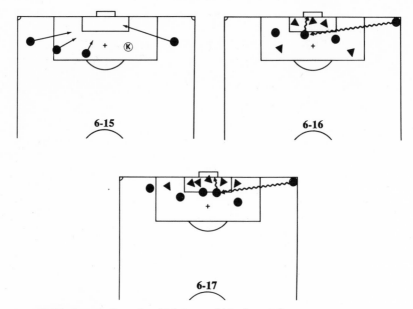

6-15

6-16

6-17

(6-15) *On an indirect free kick from within the penalty area, the kicker usually passes off to a forward who either shoots the goal or sends a pass to a teammate.* (6-16) *This corner kick is a lob to a forward stationed by the far post, who heads the ball goalward.* (6-17) *This corner kick travels low and hard to a forward by the near post; then he shoots.*

either shoots or passes off (Diagram 6–15). On the kick, the defensive players bolt from the goal to thwart the shot that usually follows the pass.

Corner Kicks   The traditional corner kick is a lob that drops down at a point six to twelve yards from the far post, and then is headed by a forward (Diagram 6–16). Nowadays, however, many teams prefer short corner kicks, and the low hard pass to a forward by the near post is quite popular (Diagram 6–17).

98

Penalty Kicks   Only the goalkeeper can defend on a kick taken from the penalty spot, but players on both teams (stationed as shown in Diagram 6–18) should be alert to charge into the penalty area for a possible rebound.

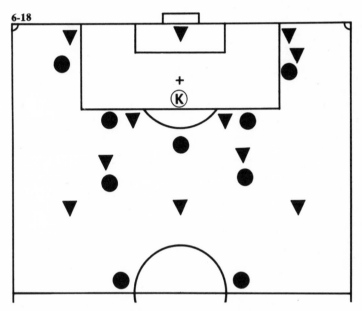

6-18   *This is how players on both teams line up on a penalty kick. The players closest to the goal are ready to bolt into the penalty area to corral a possible rebound.*

Goal Kicks   Every goal kick should be turned into a scoring thrust, with every player on the kicking team having a specific assignment. Frequently the ball is kicked as a lead pass to one of the forwards, preferably one of the outside forwards (Diagram 6–19). Well-coached teams employ a signal system

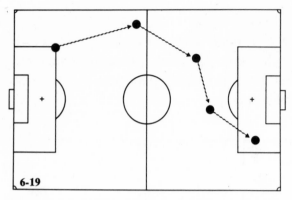

6-19 *The goal kick should always trigger a scoring attempt. In this example, the outside left receives the kick; then pass by pass the ball is worked downfield.*

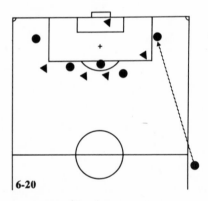

6-20 *On this touchline kick, the fullback boots to a forward upfield. He seldom, if ever, will cross the ball.*

so that players will know where the ball is going, with numbers indicating passing "lanes" or receivers.

Touchline Kicks When a touchline kick is taken by an offensive team from deep within its own territory, the kicker should seek to get the ball to a forward far upfield on the side closest to the touch-line (Diagram 6–20). When a touchline kick is taken in the area between the halfway line and the front line of the defending team's penalty area, it should be played in much the same fashion as a direct kick. And when the touchline kick is taken from a point near one of the corners, it should be played as a corner kick.

DEFENSIVE PLAY   Soccer, like basketball, features two basic defensive techniques—the man-to-man method and zone defense. Most teams use one system or the other, but there's a definite trend toward using both in combination.

Junior teams normally employ a man-to-man defense. Each defensive player covers or "marks" a particular attacking player. Usually the two fullbacks cover the opposition outside forwards. The center halfback marks the opposing center forward, and the halfbacks guard the opposing inside forwards.

The defensive man keeps within three or four yards of the enemy player, but if his man is particularly fast on his feet, the defenseman is likely to move closer. He also keeps a tighter rein on the enemy player whenever the ball gets near the penalty area.

The center halfback has to be particularly alert, always watchful for a break down the middle. He must never allow himself to be drawn farther forward than his teammates who are flanking him.

Quick switching, that is, the exchanging of defensive responsibilities with one's teammate, is vital to a successful defense. Suppose an attacking inside forward eludes his defensive man, the halfback. The fullback must move up to cover. Immediately, the halfback must circle in back of the play, providing additional protection.

If the attacking team uses a fluid style of play, with the forwards interchanging positions constantly, a zone defense is usually called for. This puts each defenseman in charge of a particular area of the field, and he covers any attacker who enters that area. Some teams use a zone defense only when the ball is upfield, but switch to a man-to-man setup in the critical area around the goal.

When opposing the 4-3-3 or 4-2-4 formations (Diagrams 6–1 and 6–2), a team should utilize four men in the final line of defense. These men should include the two fullbacks, the center halfback, and one of the outside halfbacks.

Defensemen should keep in mind that there is nothing wrong with retreating before an attack. Sometimes it can be more effective than tackling. By dropping back, a defender can slow down an attacker, allowing his teammates to get into position. Of course, when the enemy gets within shooting range of the goal, a tackle is the logical play.

Each defensive player must have a clear understanding of how to position himself on various free kick and penalty kick situations. These are shown in Diagrams 6–12 through 6–20.

CHAPTER SEVEN

PRACTICE DRILLS

As a member of the New York Generals of the North American Soccer League, I've visited most of the large cities of the United States, and wherever I travel I'm always amazed at how frequently I see youngsters practicing baseball and football. Even in downtown areas, you can usually spot a game of catch in progress. In the fall there seems to be a touch football game on every vacant lot. If American boys were to apply this same diligence to soccer practice, I'm sure they would soon equal or surpass youngsters in other parts of the world in soccer skill.

Almost all American sports are hand-oriented, and American boys usually find it strange to use their feet for both balance and ball control. But diligent practice can help to make these skills more natural for you. One of the advantages of soccer is that you can practice the game's fundamentals all by yourself. You don't need other players—not even one other—as you do when practicing the basics of football or baseball.

You must be in top-notch physical condition if you want to play soccer and play it well. Being physically sound is also good protection against injury.

Running is one of the best conditioning exercises for the game, but you should also perform exercises that will strengthen your ankle, knee, stomach, and chest muscles. The President's Council on Physical Fitness has prepared a booklet that is valuable in this regard. Entitled, *Vigor,* it instructs how to perform a variety of physique-building exercises, and features a chart to help you check your progress. The booklet costs 25 cents and is available from the Superintendent of Documents, U. S. Government Printing Office, Washington, D.C., 20402. Of course, muscle building, and fitness in general, should not be your concern only during the soccer season. Conditioning is of year-round importance.

If you're a candidate for a position on your school team, your coach will arrange a teaching program that involves both drill work on the fundamentals plus scrimmages—informal games played between two units of the team. The suggestions in the paragraphs that follow are meant to supplement the coach's advice, or, if you're not a part of a supervised training and instruction program, they can serve as the basis for a development program of your own making.

Your first practice sessions should be devoted exclusively to ball control. Any prospective player can control the ball when walking or running slowly

Soccer team candidates listen to the coach.

and in a straight line. But it's not so easy when you turn on the speed and swerve and change direction.

One useful drill is to advance slowly with the ball at your feet; gradually increase your speed, always keeping the ball in control, that is, within playing distance of your feet. When you reach a good rate of speed, stop and start every twenty-five yards. The ability to stop dead with the ball while running at full speed is extremely important in eluding tacklers.

Another good drill in learning ball control involves placing a row of six or seven three-foot stakes in the ground about six feet apart. Run in and out of the stakes a few times, first in one direction and then in the other, without the ball. Notice how rapidly you move. Now try it with the ball at your feet. If you have a stopwatch, keep a record of your time. Check periodically for improvement. If you have a partner to work with, set up two rows of stakes, then have a race. There's nothing like competition to bring out the best in a player.

Also practice dribbling in a circular pattern, first clockwise, then counterclockwise. Practice using just the inside of your feet, then the outside.

Kicking drills are of almost equal importance. If you've never played soccer, shadow-kick the basic kicking motions at first. Your first kicks using a ball should be quite short; increase the distance gradually. And always have a target when you kick.

Practice kicking with the right and the left foot. Try this exercise: From a standing position with both feet together, take a step with your left foot, then with your right foot, then left, then hop on your left, then kick the ball with your right. Then reverse the procedure—step right, step left, step right, hop right, then kick left. Kick the ball toward a wall so that it will rebound to you. Aim for a target on the wall.

Practice kicking a ball that's rolling toward you. If you're not working with a partner, rebound the ball off a wall. Have the ball come to you at various speeds, and also at various heights so that you can practice half volley and volley kicks.

106

Practice kicking the ball at different heights and speeds.

To a degree, your kicking practice should be related to the position you want to play. If you plan to be a fullback, you should work on the clearing kick, booming the ball off your instep. Mark off a four-foot circle on the field and try to drop the kick within its bounds. If you're a candidate for a half-back's post, you must be skilled in a variety of kicks, including the clearing kick.

A forward, particularly an outside forward, should be adept at dribbling downfield, then smartly crossing the ball. All forwards must work on their dribbling and shooting. When you dribble, practice swerving to the right and left. Seldom will you have a chance to drive in straight on under game conditions.

If you're strictly right-footed, concentrate on developing kicking skill with your left foot. One method is to use only the left in some kicking drills and scrimmages.

When practicing passing, always concentrate on accuracy. Pass to a partner, to a target on the wall, or a marker on the field. When working with a partner,

Practice passing with a teammate.

pass the ball back and forth while running up and down the field. Vary your passes; some should be fast; some slow; others long or short. Switch sides with your partner occasionally so that you're not always kicking with the same foot.

To practice trapping, get a partner to throw the ball to you at various speeds and heights. Use your chest, stomach, thigh, the inside and outside of your foot, and the sole of your shoe. After trapping, quickly kick the ball back to the thrower. You can practice trapping by yourself by rebounding the ball off a wall or fence. One boy I knew used to rebound the ball off a fieldstone wall. The advantage was that he never quite knew how the ball was going to rebound.

Practice heading. You can practice by yourself, simply bouncing the ball from your forehead straight up into the air. It's best if you have a partner, however. One boy throws the ball; the other heads it back. Practice sending the ball sideward and backward as well as forward. Head for distance, too.

There's nothing complicated about practice for a goalkeeper, once he's mastered the fundamentals of stopping the ball. He takes up his post and then a partner rolls, throws, or kicks balls into the goalmouth. They should come in at a variety of speeds and an assortment of angles.

A goalkeeper can also practice by throwing or kicking the ball against a wall and handling the rebound as if it were a shot. Playing basketball helps a goalie improve his skills, too. Surely one of the best

Practice heading. Keep your eyes on the ball.

ways for a goalie to sharpen his ability as a ball handler
is for him to take up his position in the goal and have
two of his teammates throw balls in from a distance

of about twelve feet, varying the speed and height at which the balls are delivered. This type of practice can make a goalkeeper as nimble as a jackrabbit.

If you're a member of a soccer team, your coach will probably set up a number of special drills involving you and several of your teammates. There will be the two-on-one drill, where two offensive players seek to work the ball past one defensive man using passes and feints. Three-on-one drills are also common.

Outside forwards often practice together. One brings the ball down the left side of the field, then sends a crossing pass to the other boy who is driving in toward the goal from the right side. He traps the ball and shoots, or shoots off the pass.

Sometimes the outside forwards practice switches with the inside forwards. Defensive switching drills are also common.

These kinds of drills are important in helping a player to meet various game situations. They're fun and they're exciting. But, as a beginner, your foremost concern should be the fundamental aspects of the game—controlling the ball, kicking it accurately, trapping, and heading. These are the foundation of any player's game, and unless they're mastered, your success—and your enjoyment, too—will be sorely limited.

In many foreign countries, the first gift a boy receives from his father is a soccer ball. And from that time on it is seldom far away from him. While

A two-on-one drill

American youngsters are frequently bussed to school, the foreign boy usually walks, and often he has a soccer ball at his feet, dribbling it as he goes. He never stops trying to improve his skills. Practice is a lifetime must if you want to succeed in the sport.

CHAPTER EIGHT

HISTORY OF SOCCER

Soccer's beginnings are too remote and too vague to be discerned by even the most diligent of historians. After all, there is nothing particularly ingenious or unusual about kicking a round object with one's foot.

But it is known that soccer, in one form or another, is one of the oldest—if not *the* oldest—sport known to mankind. About 2,500 years ago, the Chinese played a game called *tsu chu,* which means, "to kick a ball of leather with the foot." The goal was a pair of bamboo poles with a silk net strung in between. The object was to kick the hair-filled ball over the net or through a hole in it.

The early Greeks had a game in which a small ball, an inflated oval like a present-day football, was used, and players of one team had to carry the ball over a line that was defended by the other. The Romans played a spirited version of the game called *harpastum,* using the inflated bladder of a cow or horse as the ball.

Roman soldiers undoubtedly introduced soccer to England. The game was known in Chester and Darby as early as the third century. By the fourteenth century, the game was so popular, it became the subject of official wrath. On April 13, 1314, Edward II issued a proclamation forbidding soccer. "Forasmuch as there is great noise in the city caused by hustling over large balls from which many evils might arise which God forbid," the documents stated, "we commend and forbid, on behalf of the king, on pain of imprisonment, such game to be used in the city in future."

The edict was less than effective, for soon again soccer was regarded as a national menace. In 1349, Edward III objected to the game because it interfered with the practice of archery, a sport vital to the country's security. Soccer was dubbed an "idle practice," and local sheriffs were commanded to suppress it. But it might have been easier to ban the drinking of tea; the English would not give it up. Richard II, Henry IV, and Henry VIII reenacted Edward's legislation, but with a similar lack of success.

Soccer of these early times bore little resemblance to the sport we know today. The game was rather like a war, but without guns or bullets. Games were played in village streets, from one end of the town to the other, and the goals could be miles apart. Hundreds of players were on each side, and a game could last all day and into the night. Everything went —kicking, gouging, charging, tripping. One observer of the day described it as a "bloodie and murthering practice rather than a fellowy sport or pastime."

For centuries, the game was synonymous with violence. During the 1700's, an observer from France watched a game and commented, "If this is what Englishmen call playing, it would be impossible to describe what they call fighting." In addition to being quite savage, the game was also poorly organized. Few people agreed on how many players constituted a team. The playing field could be of almost any size, and the ball varied in size, shape, and even content.

Then more confusion came. In 1823, William Ellis, a student at Rugby College, unable to advance the ball by kicking it, picked it up and ran with it. Ellis might as well have stolen the crown jewels, for he was sternly rebuked. In time, however, opinions changed, and many players decided that running with the ball wasn't such a bad idea. A new game— called "rugby," of course—came into being, and Ellis became a hero.

Rugby soon attained widespread popularity. As a result, whenever the word football was used, someone was sure to ask, "What kind?"

The problem was not solved until 1863. That year those who wanted the foot kept in football formed an organization they called the London Football Association. To distinguish between the two forms of football then being played, they designated one as "rugby" and the other as "association." The word was abbreviated to become "assoc" and, ultimately, became "soccer," which shows what the passage of time can do to a word.

Soccer was introduced to the United States in the 1830's, but for decade after decade most people hardly noticed its existence. During the 1870's and 1880's, competition consisted mostly of pickup games between teams of Scotch, Irish, and English immigrants. Little by little, interest built as immigrant groups in such cities as New York, Chicago, St. Louis, Detroit, Cincinnati, and Cleveland developed teams. But, as compared to other sports, soccer's growth was slow-paced, chiefly because American youngsters looked upon it as a "foreign" game. Baseball, basketball, and football had more appeal, and soccer was shunted aside.

In 1904, soccer's chief governing body, the Fédération Internationale de Football Association, was founded. The FIFA maintains headquarters in Zürich, Switzerland.

The United States Soccer Football Association, which governs the sport in this country, was established in 1913. The organization represents the United States in the FIFA, fosters increased participation in soccer at every age level, and seeks constantly to elevate the standards of playing, coaching, and officiating. Each year the U.S.S.F.A. conducts national championship competition for the U.S. Challenge Cup, the National Amateur Cup, and the National Junior Cup. (Junior Cup champions are listed on page 120.)

116

Intercollegiate soccer is supervised by the Intercollegiate Soccer Football Association. In Canada, the Dominion of Canada Football Association is the governing body.

In recent years soccer has shown rapid development. Hundreds upon hundreds of grammar schools, high schools, and colleges have been won over to the game. Nearly every state has youth leagues. Experts agree that soccer's future has never been brighter.

Information on how to organize a team and other helpful data may be obtained from the U.S.S.F.A., Youth Promotion Committee, 79 West Monroe Street, Chicago, Illinois 60603.

OLYMPIC SOCCER Soccer football, as it's referred to in Olympic competition, made its debut on the Olympic Games program in 1900, when Great Britain won the championship. Usually, about fifty nations enter teams, however, this number is reduced to sixteen finalists by means of elimination tournaments held in various geographical zones.

In 1968, the United States was eliminated in one of the preliminary matches. The United States made its best showing in 1904, reaching the final match, but lost to Canada, 4-0.

The field of sixteen finalists is divided into four groups, and each group conducts a round robin series. The group winners advance to the semifinal match; the winner of Group 1 meets the winner of Group 2, and the winner of Group 3 meets the winner of Group 4. The winners of these matches then compete for the championship. The losers play for third place honors.

Olympic soccer matches are 90 minutes in length, with a five minute intermission between the 45-minute halves. The Olympic soccer field measures 68 meters by 105 meters.

OLYMPIC SOCCER CHAMPIONS

1900	GREAT BRITAIN	1940	(NO COMPETITION)
1904	CANADA	1944	(NO COMPETITION)
1908	GREAT BRITAIN	1948	SWEDEN
1912	GREAT BRITAIN	1952	HUNGARY
1920	BELGIUM	1956	RUSSIA
1924	URUGUAY	1960	YUGOSLAVIA
1928	URUGUAY	1964	HUNGARY
1932	(NO COMPETITION)	1968	HUNGARY
1936	ITALY		

THE WORLD CUP   Soccer has a Super Bowl and World Series all rolled into one in the World Cup Tournament, held quadrennially in even years when the Olympic Games are not scheduled. Because competition is not limited to solely amateur players, the World Cup championship is rated greater in both prestige and glory, than any other, even the Olympic title.

World Cup competition is conducted by the Fédération Internationale de Football Association. Victory is symbolized by the Jules Rimet trophy, which was first presented in 1930 to Uruguay. Teams compete in sectional playoffs to determine the qualifiers who will participate in the final rounds. In most cases, the field is reduced to sixteen teams for the final tournament.

North American teams have not fared well in World Cup competition. The United States' best showing came in 1950 when the American team scored a stunning upset in defeating England, 1-0. But the Americans were promptly eliminated in the round that followed.

When England won the World Cup in 1966, defeating West Germany in the final match, people rejoiced almost as they did on V-E Day, near the end of World War II. Trafalgar Square was jammed like Times Square on New Year's Eve. Pubs opened ahead of time and didn't close. People everywhere pranced in the streets waving the British flag. Probably no other single event in world history received such widespread coverage. Television and radio broadcast the competition to an audience of 400 million people in Europe, Asia, Africa, and North and South America.

The 1970 World Cup competition generated even greater excitement. Led by the incredible Pelé, who scored one goal and set up three, Brazil crushed Italy, 4-1, in the final match, a victory that triggered traffic-stopping celebrations in Mexico City where the final matches were held, and in virtually every city in Brazil. New York City's tiny Brazilian colony samba-danced in the streets outside Madison Square

Garden where the final game was shown on closed-circuit television.

In Italy, an estimated 35 million people watched their country's losing effort on television, and an estimated 600 to 900 million people watched worldwide. When the Brazilian team returned home, they were entertained by the President of the country.

WORLD CUP CHAMPIONS

1930	URUGUAY	1950	URUGUAY
1934	ITALY	1954	WEST GERMANY
1938	ITALY	1958	BRAZIL
1942	(NO COMPETITION)	1962	BRAZIL
1946	(NO COMPETITION)	1966	GREAT BRITAIN
		1970	BRAZIL

NATIONAL JUNIOR CUP WINNERS

1935 RELIABLE STORES; NEW BEDFORD, MASS.

1936 HATIKVOH F. C.; BROOKLYN

1937 HATIKVOH F. C.; BROOKLYN

1938 LIGHTHOUSE; PHILADELPHIA

1939 AVELLA F. C.; PA.

1940 AVELLA F. C.; PA.

1941 MERCERVILLE; TRENTON, N.J.

1942 (NO COMPETITION)

1943 (NO COMPETITION)

1944 (NO COMPETITION)

*1945 POMPEI; BALTIMORE
HORNETS; CHICAGO

120

1946	SCHUMACHER; ST. LOUIS
1947	HEIDELBERG; PA.
1948	LIGHTHOUSE B. C.; PHILADELPHIA
1949	LIGHTHOUSE B. C.; PHILADELPHIA
1950	HARRISON B.C.; N.J.
1951	SECO B.C.; ST. LOUIS
*1952	KOLLSMAN S. C.; BROOKLYN LIONS; CHICAGO
*1953	NEWARK; N.J. HANSA; CHICAGO
1954	HANSA; CHICAGO
*1955	GOTTSCHEE; NEW YORK SCHWABEN; CHICAGO
*1956	ST. ENGLEBERT; ST. LOUIS HEIDELBERG; PA.
1957	LIGHTHOUSE; PHILADELPHIA
1958	ST. PAUL; ST. LOUIS
1959	UKRAINIAN; NEW YORK
1960	ST. PAUL; ST. LOUIS
1961	HAKOAH; SAN FRANCISCO
1962	SCHUMACHERS; ST. LOUIS
1963	KUTIS; ST. LOUIS
1964	KUTIS; ST. LOUIS
1965	I. H. HEART OF MARY; ST. LOUIS
1966	ST. WILLIAM; ST. LOUIS
1967	LIGHTHOUSE; PHILADELPHIA
1968	ST. PHILIP NERI; ST. LOUIS
1969	ST. PHILIP NERI; ST. LOUIS
1970	ST. BARTS C.Y.C.; ST. LOUIS

*JOINT CHAMPION

SOCCER TERMS

BACK-UP In defensive play, when one player trails a teammate to give assistance when needed.

CENTER KICK A kick from the touchlines which goes to the center of the field in position for a goal.

CLEARING KICK A kick that sends the ball away from one's own goal toward an opponent's.

CORNER KICK A free kick from the corner area. When a defender is the last man to touch the ball before it goes out of bounds over the goal line, the attacking team is awarded a corner kick to put the ball in play. It is taken from the corner closest to where the ball crossed the goal line.

CROSS A kick that sends the ball from one side of the playing field to the other.

DIRECT FREE KICK A free kick on which a goal may be scored directly. It is awarded as a result of a personal foul such as kicking, tripping, pushing, or holding, and is taken from the spot of the infraction.

DROPPED BALL   Ball dropped by the referee to restart play after the game has been stopped for something besides a foul or goal.

FIRST TIME KICK   Kicking a ball which was not trapped.

GOAL AREA   The rectangular-shaped area immediately in front of a goal; it measures 6 yards in depth, and 20 yards in width.

GOAL KICK   When an attacking player is the last to touch the ball before it goes out of bounds across the defending team's goal line, a goal kick is awarded the defending team. The ball is placed down in the half of the goal area nearest to where it crossed the goal line.

GOAL LINE   Boundary line at each end of the field.

INDIRECT FREE KICK   A free kick, but one on which no goal can be scored directly; the ball must first be touched by another player. It is awarded for infractions that pertain primarily to violations of the playing rules, such as ungentlemanly conduct, delay of the game, and offside. The kick is awarded from the spot of the infraction.

OFFSIDE   A player is ruled offside if he is nearer his opponent's line than the ball at the moment the ball is played. A player cannot be ruled offside if he is in his own half of the field, when there are two opponents nearer to the goal line than he is, or in cases where the ball last touched an opponent or was played by him. There are no offsides on a corner kick, goal kick, throw-in, or when the ball is dropped by the referee.

PENALTY AREA   An area 18 yards in depth and 44 yards in width that encompasses the goal. The goalie is permitted the use of his hands only when within this area.

PENALTY KICK   A direct free kick awarded to a team when the opposition commits a personal foul within the penalty area. The kick is taken from the penalty mark, a point 12 yards in front of the goal, with only the goalkeeper defending.

SAVE   A stop of a goal-bound shot by a goalkeeper or opposing player.

SWITCH   When one player exchanges field position with another.

TOUCHLINE   Sideline, the boundary line on each side of the field.

THROW-IN   When a ball goes out of bounds over a sideline, it is thrown-in to play from the spot where it crossed the line. The throw-in is awarded to the opponents of the team that last touched the ball. The thrower must use a two hand over-the-head throw with both feet remaining on the ground and completely outside the field of play.

GEORGE KIRBY and GEORGE SULLIVAN

ABOUT THE AUTHORS

SOCCER is the product of a collaboration between George Kirby, a veteran of sixteen seasons in professional soccer in England and the United States, and George Sullivan, a nationally known sports writer.

From Kenilworth, England, Mr. Kirby was the star center forward with the New York Generals of the North American Soccer League. He was the team's leading scorer during 1967, with fourteen goals in eighteen games. The following season, although hampered by injuries, he scored nine goals, second highest total on the team.

Mr. Kirby's career in soccer began at the age of fifteen when he joined Everton, one of England's Division I teams. Still a schoolboy, he managed to combine his studies and soccer by attending night coaching and training sessions at the team's training camp.

He became a professional at the age of seventeen; five years later he made his debut as a major league player. He remained with Everton for ten years. In his best season, he appeared in thirty-two games and scored twelve goals.

After Everton, Mr. Kirby moved to Sheffield for a year and then to Plymouth where he made over one hundred first-team appearances and earned a reputation as one of England's most consistent goal scorers. For that reason, his services were sought by many clubs, including teams representing the newly formed leagues in the United States.

He is a rugged player, has good all-around ability, and

is particularly skilled in heading the ball. Some observers regard him as the best forward in American professional soccer. He is thirty-three years old.

Mr. Kirby, his wife, and their two children reside on Long Island, New York, during the American soccer season, returning to England in the fall. Mr. Kirby operates a real estate firm near London. His hobbies are golf, squash, and chess.

George Sullivan is the author of a good-sized shelf of books for young people, covering a wide variety of subjects. Many of them are sports-instruction books. His weekly sports-instruction column for the *Los Angeles Times* Syndicate appears in newspapers in every section of the country.

Born in Lowell, Massachusetts, Mr. Sullivan attended public schools in Springfield. He graduated from Fordham University in 1952 with a Bachelor of Science Degree. He recently joined the faculty of the Evening College, Fordham University, teaching non-fiction writing. He is a member of the Authors League of America.

Mr. Sullivan lives in New York City with his wife and son, Timothy.